HADRIAN

EMPEROR OF ROME

Leaders of the Ancient World™

HADRIAN
EMPEROR OF ROME

BEATRIZ SANTILLIAN AND
JULIAN MORGAN

Rosen YA™
NEW YORK

Published in 2018 by The Rosen Publishing Group, Inc.
29 East 21st Street, New York, NY 10010

First Edition

Library of Congress Cataloging-in-Publication Data

Names: Santillian, Beatriz, author. | Morgan, Julian, 1958- author.
Title: Hadrian : emperor of Rome / Beatriz Santillian and Julian Morgan.
Description: First edition. | New York : Rosen Publishing, 2018. | Series: Leaders of the ancient world | Includes bibliographical references and index. | Audience: Grades 7–12.
Identifiers: LCCN 2016053652 | ISBN 9781508174844 (library bound)
Subjects: LCSH: Hadrian, Emperor of Rome, 76-138—Juvenile literature. | Emperors—Rome—Biography—Juvenile literature. | Rome—History—Hadrian, 117-138—Juvenile literature.
Classification: LCC DG295 .S24 2018 | DDC 937/.07092 [B] —dc23
LC record available at https://lccn.loc.gov/2016053652

Manufactured in China

On the cover: Ancient Roman sculpture of the emperor Hadrian.

CONTENTS

INTRODUCTION

After 482 years of rule by the people, the Republic of Rome evolved (or dissolved) into an empire with a complex system of interweaving governments, ones that each new emperor had to reconcile in order to remain in control. With these changes in regime, the global environment had to be manipulated into both a unified and malleable entity time and time again. Sometimes, such manipulation came at the hands of harsh violence, like stamping out the many religiously provoked Jewish rebellions. Other times, simply administering certain protections like

strengthening a frontier made all the difference in protecting the Roman Empire from invasion. In the midst of being an international entity with such burdens, an emperor's death often led to a scramble for power in which enemies of emerging figures were purged, and the people came to fear tyranny.

Amid this backdrop, the Five Good Emperors, rulers who would ascend to the throne by adoption, would make themselves known for what is often perceived as a less harsh rule. Publius Aelius Hadrianus became the third of

These busts depict the Five Good Emperors of Rome. From left to right, they are Nerva, Trajan, Hadrian, Antoninus Pius, and Marcus Aurelius. They lived between 30 and 180 CE.

those emperors immediately after being adopted by Trajan. His twenty-one years of rule would encompass diplomacy in adversity and building up the infrastructure of the empire during peace.

Except for when it didn't. The disastrous revolt of Bar Kokhba left hundreds of thousands dead, with each side suffering massive losses. Hadrian's years of traveling and leaving his mark on the empire would culminate in a prolonged act of dominance that showed the true might of an empire, as well as its vulnerabilities.

As with other ancient civilizations, the sources that were available to tell of Hadrian's life consisted of biographies and archaeological evidence that either survived or were alluded to in a written work. The many statues of Hadrian sprinkled around the territory once known as the Roman Empire paint a picture of a man who wanted to be ubiquitous, whereas the absence of his name from the buildings he had erected conflicts with that notion. Writings about his inability to maintain healthy relationships with his companions suggest some aberration in personality, while his diplomatic approach to potential crises of government rule throughout the empire suggest that he could be relatable when he wanted to be.

And then there is what he left behind. Between the civil wars and foreign invasions that followed Hadrian and the following two Good Emperors, the Roman Empire seemed to become more about self-preservation than expansion. And he was the first to encourage that attitude. The tide of history began to turn, following on the heels of his own reforms, but ancient Rome would never be forgotten.

Hadrian could easily be judged as a hero or as a villain for his acts. His fear of the people around him indicated that he was already subjected to such judgement during his lifetime, and that fear also indicates that he may have deserved it. This examination of his life offers nothing in the way of asserting such an interpretation, but simply presents the history that has emerged.

CHAPTER 1

THE RISE OF HADRIAN

The landscape of Roman politics gave any patrician the chance to rise to the highest ranks. But like any institution, there were elements of politics that would help some contenders float toward the top in a faster and easier manner. The story of Hadrian's rise is one such case.

HADRIAN'S ORIGINS

Hadrian was born on January 24, 76 CE, though whether he was born in Spain or in Rome is unclear. His father, Hadrianus Afer, was a senator and a praetor who came from the Spanish town of Italica, now known as Santiponce, near Seville. His mother, Paulina, came from Gades, now known as Cadiz. The family was rich and important, with estates in Italica and Rome. Hadrian's father was the cousin of Trajan, who became emperor in 97 CE. When Hadrianus Afer died, Hadrian was about ten years old, and Trajan became his guardian, along with another man, Publius Acilius Attianus. Hadrian may have spent some of his childhood in Rome and some of it in Spain. An early friendship was formed between Trajan's wife, Plotina, and Hadrian, who also got to know and admire Matidia, Trajan's niece. At the age of about fourteen, Hadrian put on a man's toga for the first time, an event that marked his new legal status as an adult, and he visited Italica to look over his estates. He then took an active part in the local association of wealthy young men, developing a keen interest in hunting.

Later, in the year 90 CE, Hadrian came to Rome under the wing of Trajan. He continued his education, and in 94 CE became a *vigintivir* (twenty man), one of twenty officials in Rome chosen from the young nobles to serve for one year in minor official capacities. This was the first rung on the *cursus honorum*, which was very well defined for the sons of upper-class Romans. In this capacity, he served in the courts as an attendant, learning the crafts of law and public speaking. He was also

THE CURSUS HONORUM

Four main magistracy posts make up the cursus honorum. The chronological order in which these posts would be held is quaestor, aedile, praetor, and consul. Two of the eight quaestors were expected to serve as assistants to the consuls, while others were financial administrators. Four aediles maintainted the city and food of Rome and facilitated in the games and festivals. Those eight men who held the role of praetor dealt with domestic matters, transnational matters within the empire, and provincial matters. And finally, two consuls would direct the military, oversee Senate proceedings, introduce laws, and veto inappropriate actions by the other consul. Each of these positions lasted a year and were elected by either the *comitia tributa*, the *concilium plebis*, or the *comitia centuriata*.

chosen to preside in the city during times of public holiday and celebration.

HADRIAN ENTERS MILITARY SERVICE

Hadrian was selected in 95 CE to become a military tribune in a legion. He went to serve in the

This illustration is of a fifth-century Roman Empire military tribune. Hadrian would serve as a military tribune on several occasions.

second legion at Aquincum (modern-day Budapest) in Pannonia, on the Danube River. The second legion, called Adiutrix, had recently seen service in Britain, and it is possible that Hadrian had conversations with soldiers even at that time about the northern frontiers of the Roman Empire. Unusual for the time, Hadrian went on to a second and even a third term as military tribune, with the fifth legion (Macedonia) in Oescus, in modern-day Bulgaria, and later with the twenty-second legion (Primigenia) in Moguntiacum, now called Mainz, in Germany. During this time, the hated emperor Domitian was killed in Rome in 96 CE and Nerva acceded to power. He in turn died in early 98 CE, some time after adopting Trajan as his heir. Hadrian seized the opportunity to take news of the aged emperor's death to Trajan in Colonia Agrippinensis (modern-day Cologne).

Hadrian had a sister, Domitia Paulina, who had married an important Roman called Lucius Julius Servianus. Servianus was presently governor of Upper Germany, where Hadrian was tribune. Hadrian and Servianus seem to have gotten along badly at this time. Servianus is known to have complained to Trajan about the young man's extravagance and his excessive desire for hunting. At this stage it is likely that Trajan worried about Hadrian, since the young man had not yet earned his full confidence.

Trajan kept his position near the Danube River, keeping a watchful eye on the Sarmatian and Dacian tribes, who lived north of the river in modern-day Romania. Servianus became governor of Pannonia (Hungary), close to the river, which acted as a frontier at that time. In late 99 CE, however, Trajan returned to Rome to be acclaimed emperor and among his followers was the young Hadrian.

Trajan and Hadrian had a quarrel at this time, which led to a cooling down between them. But in spite of their differences, the empress Plotina continued to support Hadrian, finding him a wife in 100 CE, when he was twenty-four years old. Sabina Augusta was the daughter of Plotina's friend and the emperor's niece, Matidia, whom Trajan regarded almost as a daughter, so a close family link was preserved. Hadrian and Sabina may have started off well enough, but it is clear that their marriage was a convenience, and certainly in its later stages they were not fond of each other at all.

HADRIAN'S POLITICAL PATH

After his marriage, Hadrian was elected to several positions that were steps up the cursus honorum. He first became a quaestor in 101 CE, which in turn meant that he could join the Senate. In this capacity

This photo features some influential women from Hadrian's life. In the foreground is Plotina, Trajan's wife and Hadrian's eventual adoptive mother.

he occasionally stood in to read Trajan's speeches publicly and was made fun of for his strange accent in Latin. He may perhaps have had a slight Spanish accent to his speech, as he is known to have worked on improving his pronunciation to reduce his embarrassment. Hadrian was often called "Graeculus," or little Greek, for his fascination with Greek language and literature, so he was used to teasing and strong enough not to show any discomfort over it.

Within several months of becoming quaestor, Hadrian was chosen by Trajan to join him as a member of his personal staff on the first expedition to Dacia. It was said that he became a drinking companion to the emperor, to ingratiate himself with Trajan, learn his habits, and become closer to him. This campaign is famously depicted on Trajan's Column in Rome. Roman legions marched into the area north of the Danube River in Romania to fight against the Dacian leader Decebalus, who had been causing problems for some years. Within two years Decebalus had surrendered to the Romans and peace was made, though unfortunately it would not last.

Hadrian was back in Rome by the next year, 102 CE, and was made tribune of the people. At this time, his brother-in-law Servianus was consul, one of the two chief magistrates in the city, presumably keeping an eye on the young man's progress. Three

These busts depict Sabina and her husband, Hadrian. They were married in 100 CE.

years later Hadrian became praetor, or senior magistrate. War against Decebalus was declared again, however, since the Dacian king had not abided by his agreement after the first war. Hadrian once more went off to war with Trajan, this time in charge of the first legion, to serve in the second Dacian expedition that ended a year later with the capture of Sarmizegethusa and the suicide of Decebalus. Trajan then added Dacia as a province to the Roman Empire along with Arabia, which had been acquired more peacefully.

In 107 CE, Trajan staged a set of games in Rome to celebrate the success of the Dacian campaigns. Hadrian was decorated for his role in both campaigns, and he appears by then to have earned considerable respect from Trajan and others, despite the earlier setbacks in their relationship. He was appointed governor of Pannonia Inferior and returned to Aquincum, where he had been military tribune in his first term of office. This time, however, Hadrian was the man in charge, with absolute power of life and death over his subjects. It was his job as a provincial governor to ensure that Roman laws were upheld, that military matters ran smoothly, and that the finances were kept in order.

THE FINAL RUNG

By early 108 CE, Hadrian had become *suffect* consul, thus making it to the top. Hadrian must have felt proud to achieve this position at such a young age. He was only thirty-two. When he did return to Rome, he was given the job of writing speeches for Trajan and was a member of the emperor's inner group of friends. His various skills were also becoming apparent. Hadrian was an expert singer, a player of the kithara (a kind of early guitar), a poet, a philosopher, a military engineer, and an architect. He was also a keen painter and a sculptor. His interests were so diverse that he came into contact with many leading scholars, but this did not always make him friends.

The Roman economy was booming at this time, after the Dacian campaign had brought great wealth into the city. Apollodorus the architect was instrumental in building Trajan's famous markets alongside his new forum, and he did not want to see an amateur like Hadrian moving in on his territory, telling the young man to get back to his still-life sketches. One day the two argued while discussing his plans for the city and its port, Ostia.

Apollodorus felt confident in rejecting young Hadrian's advice, but it was an argument Hadrian never forgot.

After his consulship, Hadrian decided to embark on a tour that would take him away from Rome for the next eight years. He would not return until becoming emperor. As the former "Graeculus," Hadrian wanted to see his beloved Greece, and his path took him first to Athens. Here he fit in so well with Athenian society that he was made an honorary Athenian citizen and even became the eponymous archon in the year 112 CE. This meant that the Athenians had chosen him as their chief magistrate. This was of course only ceremonial, as Athens was by then just another part of the Roman Empire and not an independent state. It was at this time that Hadrian began to spread his influence in other ways too. He grew a beard in the Greek style, which had not been commonplace among earlier Romans. Hadrian's beard would affect generations to come, creating a new fashion for his countrymen.

Some time after this, Trajan appeared in Athens on his way to the eastern empire and Parthia. Conflicts had broken out there that required his

This painting of Hadrian depicts the Greek style of beard, which wasn't commonly adopted by Romans until his rise to power.

personal attention. Again he recruited his young adviser to follow him. The campaign brought the two men to Syria, Armenia, Mesopotamia, and even as far as Babylon, but this was the campaign that cost Trajan his life.

DEATH AND ASCENSION

Trajan had been on his way home, worn out and ill after his efforts in the eastern part of the empire. His capture of the Parthian capital Ctesiphon in 116 CE had seemed to bring a successful close to a four-year campaign. Hadrian had been one of his trusted staff officers. For his efforts Trajan had received the titles imperator (conquering general) and Parthicus. However, the Roman Empire, larger than it had ever been, was suffering strains. Trajan sacrificed to the ghost of Alexander the Great at Babylon before he heard that rebellions were breaking out in Cyprus, Egypt, and Libya, as well as in Dacia and Mesopotamia where his recent successes had been gained. The great warrior emperor, who had seen himself as a second Alexander the Great, must have been broken in spirit to hear that his new conquests were already causing such problems. He probably left Ctesiphon a bitter man.

Trajan knew he was ill. He had suffered a stroke and partial paralysis, but following the example of his hero Alexander, he had chosen no clear successor. He had appointed Hadrian consul *ordinarius,* the top politician in Rome, for the following year, 118 CE, but this in itself is not evidence that Trajan wanted him to become emperor. Trajan said that he knew of many who could become the next emperor, but he had not taken the trouble to decide who this should be. Or so it seemed, until exactly one day after his death on August 8, 117 CE. Then the news arrived in Syria that Trajan had in fact adopted Hadrian. It seems more than likely that the letter of adoption was written on the initiative of Trajan's wife, Plotina, who had always had a soft spot for Hadrian, either just before or just after the emperor breathed his last breath. Therefore many saw Hadrian's new position as dubious at best.

Did Trajan really adopt Hadrian? Whichever version of events is true, the new emperor's job was to convince the Senate, citizens, and soldiers of Rome that he was a worthy successor.

On August 11, 117 CE, at the age of forty-one, Hadrian, recently appointed as the governor of Syria, became emperor of Rome. It was a momentous time

Located in Rome, Italy, Trajan's Column is the designated location of Trajan's remains.

for the Roman Empire, especially after the popular campaigns and military expansions of the previous emperor, Trajan, who had just died in Selinus, Cilicia. Hadrian's first task was to confirm himself in his new role by receiving the acceptance of others, something he could in no way have taken for granted at that time.

CHAPTER 2

STABILIZING THE ROMAN EMPIRE

The Roman Empire was notorious for outbreaks of violence following the death of an emperor, usually when that emperor failed to choose a successor. A civil war could result from this power struggle, or the empire could simply dissolve if a strong enough leader failed to emerge. Hadrian managed to avoid both of these outcomes through what many saw as tyranny, as well as through some diplomacy and bribery.

SECURING HIS DOMAIN

Once Hadrian came to power in 117 CE, he had some serious difficulties to overcome before being accepted across the Roman Empire as its new ruler. The first of his troubles was the set of rumors that had arisen from the process by which he had gained power. It had been known for some time that Trajan had no heirs, so Hadrian's adoption just one day before the previous emperor's death looked at best suspicious and at worst deceitful. It was known that Trajan had promoted Hadrian and respected him, but also that the Empress Plotina had loved him as if he were her own son. It seemed that the new emperor owed his position more to her than to his adopted father. Others said Hadrian's former guardian Attianus was involved and that Trajan had in fact died several days earlier, and the news of the death kept quiet until Hadrian could be adopted.

Further problems faced the new emperor as a result of the general instability of the empire. Hadrian needed to take action quickly to restore order, as well as to make his own position secure. His first steps must have been seen as controversial. He proceeded immediately to abandon all Roman possessions in Mesopotamia, Assyria, and Armenia, thus undoing much of Trajan's recent work. All land gained in the region of the Tigris and Euphrates Rivers was evacuated by the Romans, and it was not long before Hadrian also abandoned much of Dacia, captured in Trajan's two great campaigns, where he himself had also played a role.

This map shows the Roman Empire before Hadrian abandoned some of the territories Trajan had won.

Hadrian sent a letter to the Senate in Rome, accompanying the old emperor's ashes, asking for the senators' pardon for assuming authority so soon and without their direct approval, while at the same time requesting that Trajan should receive divine honors and thus become a god in the Roman religion. Soon the reply came back that Hadrian's position as princeps, or first citizen, was approved.

So his first worries were allayed, but there were still more concerns for the new ruler.

Within a short time, Hadrian dismissed Lusius Quietus from his job as governor of Judea. There may have been a number of reasons for this, but it is likely that Hadrian saw Quietus first and foremost as a rival for the imperial throne. By removing him from authority, he thought he was securing his own position. The Jewish community, however, saw this differently, thinking that Hadrian was protecting them from an anti-Semitic governor who had led the Roman assault against their rebellions in Cyprus, Egypt, and Libya. Quietus came from Mauretania (Morocco) in North Africa, and by his removal Hadrian caused civil disturbances to break out in that region. Hadrian ignored the advice of Attianus to put to death as pretenders to the throne Baebius Macer, prefect of Rome, and Calpurnius Crassus Frugi. Calpurnius was killed in any case some time later on Attianus's orders. At the same time, it was reported that there were uprisings in Britain, a new external threat to Hadrian's power.

APPEALING TO THE PEOPLE

Hadrian's skill at this stage of his career seems to have been in prioritizing tasks. He addressed each of his problems in turn, realizing that he could not do everything at once. Whereas he needed to do some things in person, other situations could be trusted to colleagues. So he sent one of his most loyal, capable, and trusted friends, Marcius Turbo, to deal with affairs in Egypt and Libya. Turbo had been a centurion in Aquincum, whom Hadrian had probably met during his first posting there in 95 CE. Hadrian himself, learning that the previous governor of Dacia had died recently, set off northwards to go to this region. Before he left Syria, he stopped in a place called Daphne and took the strange step of blocking up a spring called the Castalian Spring, where apparently it had been foretold that he would be emperor. This was a symbolic act, as if to say that no other emperor would be proclaimed from that place, thus securing Hadrian's own position.

Hadrian's path took him from Syria through Thrace (now Turkey) to Anatolia, the land we now call Asia Minor. At Ancyra, he allowed himself to be identified with the god of wine and was worshipped as the new Dionysus. This may have been the first time that Hadrian allowed himself to be called a god, but it certainly was not the last. It is interesting to speculate about how much the emperor himself may have believed in his own divine status. Regardless, if Hadrian could appear as a god in the eyes of foreign people, he could gain greater authority with them. So we can see Hadrian's habit of allowing himself to be worshipped as part of his strategy to gain control over foreign peoples and achieve stability throughout the Roman Empire.

On Hadrian's arrival in Dacia, he turned first to diplomacy rather than the outright warfare that had been Trajan's method of resolving things. The Roxolani tribe occupied lands to the north of the Danube in what is now Bulgaria. They came to an agreement to split Trajan's newly acquired province, so that they could become peaceful neighbors with the Romans. The king of the tribe was made an honorary Roman citizen to confirm the agreement. Dacia itself was divided into three separate Roman provinces, taking the place of the much larger administrative unit left by Trajan.

Hadrian was probably first worshipped as a god when he took on the persona of Dionysus.

MURDER CONSPIRACY

Meanwhile, in Rome, the absent Hadrian came under attack from his enemies, who saw his abandonment of Trajan's policies as disastrous for the future of the empire. It was becoming clear to them that the new ruler did not want to expand Rome's empire any farther and that his policies would favor strengthening what Rome already had rather than gaining any more lands. Since the reign of Augustus, it was commonly believed by most Romans that the empire should continue to grow without bounds. Hadrian did not endorse this policy, creating conflict with several senior politicians. Soon, they were voicing their objections.

Hadrian made his way to Byzantium, now the city of Istanbul, where he spent some of the winter of 117/118 CE continuing to review his policies and preparing for a return journey to Rome, which he had last seen eight years before. Marcius Turbo, successful in his attempts to calm things down in Mauretania, was sent to Dacia as its new governor. This, too, must have irritated some career politicians, as Turbo had come to prominence as a soldier and had no political background at all.

Shortly afterward, four men in Italy were killed, all of the highest rank in Roman society. They were ex-consuls, supposedly involved in a conspiracy against the emperor. One of them was Lusius Quietus, the former governor of Judea removed by Hadrian. He had a history of disagreement with emperors, having fallen out of Domitian's favor years ago. Also implicated were Avidius Nigrinus, who had been dismissed from Hadrian's personal staff, Cornelius Palma, and Publilius Celsus. It seems that the conspiracy, if it was indeed such, had been discussed in the Senate, which had voted to punish the four men. The punishment was carried out by Attianus, ex-guardian of Hadrian.

On his return to Rome, after the killings of the ex-consuls, the emperor tried hard to convince his subjects that he was no tyrant. Rome had seen several excessively cruel emperors, such as Caligula, Nero, and Domitian, and the people did not want to return to an age where the first citizen's enemies mysteriously disappeared or were openly killed. Hadrian wanted to be seen as a man of the people, so he took steps to mix with them whenever he could. He did not use carriages when he could walk and did not stand on ceremony when it was unnecessary. He tried hard to distance himself from Attianus's actions and spoke about this in the Senate. Hadrian denied that the killings had been done on his orders and even sacked Attianus as prefect of the guard in Rome, a post that was then taken by Hadrian's friend and loyal supporter Marcius Turbo. Turbo would stay in this post for many years to come, and his continued presence in Rome protected the emperor's authority for much of his remaining time in power.

REFORM AND BRIBERY

As consul ordinarius for the first half of the year 118 CE, Hadrian combined the role of princeps (emperor) with that of consul (prime minister), which was a fairly normal combination at that time. However, he gave up the post of suffect consul in July so that other consuls would be allowed to take up their posts, demonstrating his willingness to fit in with the standard practice of the time.

Hadrian then made a donation of six gold pieces to all Roman citizens, who had previously received three gold pieces when he first came to the throne. This broad act of bribery of the people was an established way to gain popularity and was, Hadrian said, a way of sharing the success achieved in the provinces. Hadrian also pledged his ongoing support to the Senate and promised that he would never punish a senator without putting it first to a vote of his peers. He felt that the state, still referred to as the Republic, should belong to its Senate and the people, and not be seen as the emperor's personal property.

Hadrian also cancelled all previously existing tax debts, going back as far as fifteen years. This was a popular move, as taxation in Rome was always

ROMAN CURRENCY AND ECONOMY

Coinage of the Roman Republic consisted of two types of coins. Staters, the first type, were standard coins of various high values that were made of gold. The second type consisted of silver coins. Types of silver coins included the didrachm/denarius (plural: denarii), the *quinarus* (plural: *quinari*), the iis/*sestertius* (plural: *sestertii*), and the as (plural: asses). Using the denarius as the reference, a quinarus was 1/2 its value, a sestertius was 1/4 of the value, and an as was 1/16 of its value.

Knowing that seven to ten sestertii could buy one modius (14.7lb or 6.67 kg) of wheat and that on average people ate around four modi of bread per month establishes an index for the price of feeding the people. Meanwhile, knowing that a secretary earns sixty sestertii per month and knowing the earning power of other careers offers a reference point for both the total tax debt of the Romans and the affordability of living there. But not all people lived on bread, and prices would fluctuate frequently unless prices were fixed.

These Roman denarii are from around 117–138 CE, the period of Hadrian's reign.

problematic and at this time the money owed was a huge amount, around 900 million sesterces. Cancellation of debt on such a large scale left a massive sum of money available for spending, and Hadrian's measure boosted the Roman economy.

Further steps taken by Hadrian included a reform of the law that said that the property of condemned people should go to the emperor's purse. Instead, it would go to the public treasury. Payments to parents with children, introduced by Trajan, were raised to promote family life, so that parents received financial support for girls to age fourteen and boys to age eighteen. Hadrian also made it illegal for masters to kill their slaves, which had previously been allowed by law.

As a result of his reforms, not to mention his wholesale bribery of the people, Hadrian was suddenly more popular than he had ever been before, and his abandonment of Trajan's policies was less resented. He was called the restorer and the enricher of Rome by people who only recently denounced his domestic focus. The official deification of Trajan took place after his ashes had been installed in his column in the new forum. After this, the emperor paid for a huge gladiatorial show in Janu-

Gladiatorial shows often included scenes like this one, in which lions were let loose to kill the unfortunate victims in the arena.

ary 119 CE. It was held to celebrate his forty-third birthday, and one thousand animals were killed for the entertainment of the Roman people, including two hundred lions. This funding of public entertainment was an established way for an emperor or a leading politician to work up public support for his cause. Hadrian was consul ordinarius this year again, for the third and last time of his career.

IMPROVING ROME'S INFRASTRUCTURE

Later in the same year, Hadrian went on a journey around southern Italy, spending time in the region of Campania visiting cities whose foundations dated back to Greek times and enjoying the pleasant climate. There does not seem to have been a motive for this trip besides the obvious one of taking a holiday. At this point, he was much more at ease with himself and with his position and sought to maintain an illusion that he was just another citizen, though perhaps an elevated one. He was clearly a remarkable man, able to do many jobs at the same time, and apparently he had a phenomenal memory. It is said that he never forgot a name and could quote at length from the books he had read.

Toward the end of 119 CE, Hadrian was upset to hear of the death of his mother-in-law, Matidia, who had been a good friend to him for many years. He allowed her to be deified. It is unknown whether Matidia had helped to keep relations amiable between Hadrian and his wife, Sabina, but his affection for his mother-in-law certainly seems to have been greater than that for her daughter.

Hadrian stayed in Rome for the next year or so, devoting much of his time and energy to internal politics, but also to architecture, one of his favorite hobbies. It was at this time that he designed the Pantheon, one of the most beautiful buildings in Rome. He set plans in motion to construct a huge temple for Rome and the goddess Venus near the forum that would take many years to complete. Other projects included the

This photo depicts the interior of the Pantheon, a structure designed personally by Hadrian.

strengthening of the riverbanks of the Tiber and the restoration of many buildings.

Hadrian was modest about his accomplishments. Although it was customary for the person paying for a building to have his name inscribed on it, Hadrian's name appears on very few of the buildings he restored or built. Even the Pantheon did not have Hadrian's name written on it, though he totally redesigned and rebuilt the original construction, erected by Agrippa in the time of Augustus.

As a symbol that he would no longer seek to extend the empire, Hadrian renewed the boundary stones of the city of Rome that defined the city limits (*pomerium*). In former times it had been customary to extend the boundary of Rome when the empire grew, so Hadrian was sending a clear message to his citizens, who had perhaps by then accepted the policy of nonexpansion, seduced by a series of populist policies. As part of Hadrian's propaganda for acceptance, coins minted at this time depicted the new era as a golden age.

CHAPTER 3

FESTIVITIES AND FRONTIERS

Hadrian fulfilled his duty as emperor by strengthening the empire's hold on its various lands and beautifying many of the places he came across. There seemed to be much fun in his work, as it mostly involved travelling around and a pastime he had always cherished, designing great architectural structures. But he could not only be preoccupied with imparting strength and beauty to his empire, as he would find and lose some precious connections along the way.

FORTIFYING THE FRONTIER

Hadrian stayed in Rome until April 21, 121 CE, when a great festival was held in the city. That festival may have been designed as a grand send-off party for the emperor, who at that time chose to depart on his travels again. He had decided to survey the extent of his rule in the north and west of the empire. His journey took him through Gaul and Germany, and he inspected the military installations as he went.

The first major weakness he found in Rome's northern defenses was in the area between the Rhine and Danube Rivers in Germany. Hadrian was concerned that, wherever possible, natural features should be exploited and turned into barriers between Roman and non-Roman territory. So the huge rivers were important in delineating the frontiers of his rule. The Rhine, connecting the North Sea to Switzerland in a long north-south line, formed one strong barrier, and the Danube performed a similar function along an east-west line stretching as far as the Black Sea. Hadrian noted that the Main River, a tributary of the Rhine, was not being fully used and that the land lying between the Main and the Danube offered little protection against an enemy attack. This was where he first started to build an artificial frontier called a *limes* (pronounced lee-mez), the origin of the English word "limit." The German limes was a wall of wood, made of split wooden logs creating

This Roman watchtower was built in Germany as part of the *limes*.

a palisade. It ran between Mainz and modern-day Regensburg.

A second weakness Hadrian noted was that the Roman army had been at peace for so long in some of the frontier regions that it was losing its effectiveness and discipline. He insisted that rigorous training programs be introduced and adhered to, with soldiers practicing maneuvers, weapons training, and fitness regimes. Marches of twenty miles (thirty-two kilometers) or more in full armor were carried out and strict rules were employed for soldiers or officers who wanted to go on leave. Clear age limits were established so that soldiers could not be too young or too old. Hadrian also instituted a policy for the legions that no money should be spent on equipment that was unserviceable. Hadrian maintained that there was no use having an army unless it was ready to defend the frontiers of the empire, and his reforms of military practice became standard for many years to come. In keeping with his man-of-the-people approach, he took an active part in these exercises, sharing quarters and food with his own soldiers.

THE FRONTIER IN ENGLAND

After visiting Germany, Hadrian went to Britain in 122 CE with a newly appointed governor, Aulus Platorius Nepos. Hadrian aimed to secure a frontier system across the entire Roman world that would allow it to remain strong. But Britain did not really have an effective frontier system at all. Southern England had been occupied by the Romans in 43 CE. Agricola had been governor of the province between 78 and 84 CE, before being recalled to Rome by the emperor Domitian, and he had tried hard in that time to subdue the northern tribes, reaching as far as Scotland. Here a battle was fought at Mons Graupius, the exact location of which is still a mystery. The outcome of the fighting was not clear, however, since Agricola's enemies kept making a series of guerrilla attacks on the Roman troops. Agricola decided to move south and to consolidate a defensive system around two existing Roman roads, Dere Street and the Stanegate. The new northern frontier of the Roman Empire became a long, curving road, which did not create an adequate barrier for the frontier. Hadrian decided to

This is what remains of Hadrian's Wall, the boundary between Roman and foreign territory that was erected in Great Britain.

strengthen the line of separation between Roman and non-Roman territory by constructing a 70-mile-long (112-km-long) wall with extensive fortifications across the country.

During his time in Britain, Hadrian came into conflict with some of his close colleagues, who apparently misbehaved in some way with his wife, Sabina. The details are not known for sure, but the historian Suetonius, who was also Hadrian's private secretary, was dismissed from his staff and sent back in disgrace to Rome, together with a senior officer called Septicius Clarus. His relationship with his wife was almost certainly very poor by then, and he probably

HADRIAN'S WALL

Hadrian's Wall was and still is the largest construction project ever undertaken in Europe. Hadrian personally oversaw its design and the first part of the construction, resulting in the division between England and Scotland that still remains as a reference in modern times. However, the border has shifted many times from the line of his original wall. Its purpose was to separate the Romans from the non-Romans in Britain. It also provided a visible sign that Roman expansionism was over and that the existing empire should prioritize being contained securely.

Hadrian's Wall had one so-called mile castle and two watchtowers for each mile of its length, with forts housing five hundred or more soldiers spread out at roughly 5-mile (8-km) intervals. To the south, perhaps added after Hadrian's original plans were framed, there was a military road and a huge ditch-based system called the *vallum*, which created a kind of no-man's-land where only military personnel were allowed. The wall also had a ditch on the north side that invaders would have to climb through before being able to attack the Romans on the parapet, twenty feet (six meters) above ground level.

kept her with him on his travels for fear that she would do him harm if left alone in Rome. He once said he wished he could rid himself of her for being moody and difficult.

GRIEF IN CONTINENTAL EUROPE

Toward the end of 122 CE, Hadrian left Britain, bound for Gaul and Spain. It was en route through Gaul that his beloved horse Borysthenes died and was buried in the south of France near Nimes. Hadrian also erected a temple here to Trajan's mother, Plotina, who had recently died. Hadrian wore black clothes for nine days to mark his grief for her. Hearing of a riot in Egypt, he addressed a letter to the people there that is said to have calmed them down, and his journey continued. He spent the winter in Tarraco, in Spain, where he rebuilt the temple of Augustus. It was at that time that he began to simplify his own name to Hadrianus Augustus, and it is clear that he wanted to be seen as a second Augustus. Image was everything in the Roman world, and Hadrian sought identification with the first emperor of Rome, whose reputation remained unblemished.

This emperor who traveled so widely in his life made a curious omission from his trip to Spain. He failed to return to Italica, his own hometown. Whatever the reasons for this, he did donate generously to a building program in the town, which included a new amphitheater. Instead of visiting Italica, Hadrian went to Gades (Cadiz), his mother Paulina's hometown. During the trip to Spain, at some time in mid-123 CE, news arrived of a rebellion in Mauretania (Morocco), which Hadrian probably visited personally. Perhaps more seriously, problems resurfaced in Parthia. Hadrian then left his western empire to head east, where his rule had begun.

MOVING THROUGH ASIA MINOR

By June 123 CE, Hadrian was back with his retinue of servants and followers in Antioch, Syria. He held a summit meeting in the area of the Euphrates River with the Parthian king Chosroes and seems to have made a peaceful settlement. From here he went north to Cappadocia, where he visited another frontier system somewhat like the limes in Germany. He spent the winter in Nicomedia, in

This is a painting by Piero della Francesca of the Parthian king Chosroes, who would choose peace after becoming a threatening rival of the Roman Empire.

what is now northern Turkey. It was at this time that Hadrian met a young man called Antinous in the town of Bithynium Claudiopolis. Antinous at the time was about thirteen years old and may have been taken onto Hadrian's staff as a young retainer, accompanying him on his travels.

In the following year, 124 CE, Hadrian moved through various parts of Asia Minor, going to the great cities of Ephesus and Smyrna. He went to Rhodes, where he may have helped to restore the great Colossus, a huge statue that bestrode the harbor. Hadrian's habit was to create or promote a building project in the places he visited, something he could build or restore, demonstrating both his fascination with architecture and his passion for history—usually Greek. Another project by him on this trip was the completion of the Temple of Zeus at Cyzicus, begun three hundred years earlier. Hadrian immodestly had the building completed and dedicated jointly to Zeus and himself. He visited some famous monuments, such as the tomb of the famous Greek warrior Ajax at Troy, and on his travels he renamed many of the cities visited either Hadriane or Hadrianopolis. Thus he made a mark wherever he went that was to endure for many years to come.

In spite of Hadrian's supposed restoration efforts, the Colossus of Rhodes, depicted here in a painting, did not survive the test of time.

AN EMPEROR'S VACATION

In the autumn of 124 CE, Hadrian ended his eastern excursions with a second trip to Athens, where he realized a long-held ambition of taking part in the Eleusinian Mysteries. Participants came from the entire Greek-speaking world, so Hadrian's involvement would not have been seen as exceptional, though it was clearly a very unusual thing for an emperor to do. These celebrations had been part of Athenian society for many years and were connected with the idea that worshippers experienced something that could assure them of life after death. The ritual involved a procession of people from Athens to Eleusis, about 15 miles (24 km) west of the city. The gods worshipped in the mysteries were Dionysus and Ceres, daughter of Persephone. Ceres, or Demeter as the Romans knew her, was goddess of the crops and farming, whereas Dionysus, or Bacchus, was god of wine. A swim in the sea for purification before the procession led to the torchlight ceremony. Full initiation did not come until a person had taken part in the mysteries twice, so Hadrian must have had in mind even then that he would return. And he would, in the summer of 128 CE.

Hadrian spent some time in the city of Athens and managed to create an extra tribe, named after himself. The tribes of Athens were introduced about six hundred years earlier as part of a political system for general administration and to enable voting to take place in manageable groups. Hadrian spent time reforming the laws of this ancient and important city that had influenced so many others and had always fascinated him. He then embarked on a brief tour of southern Greece, visiting Argos and Sparta among other cities. By March of 125 CE, he was back in Athens, presiding over the Great Dionysia, the most important of all the public festivals in the city. At that time, he saw an opportunity to work on the largest of all the monuments he ever restored, the great Temple of Olympian Zeus at Athens. This undertaking had begun about six hundred year before by the tyrant of Athens, Pisistratus, but was still unfinished. Hadrian resumed work on the buildings and started work on designs for the area around the temple, the *temenos*. At the same time he began other building projects, including a new aqueduct for taking water from Mount Parnes to the center of the city. Near the agora, or city center, he also planned a library with a giant

Hadrian was highly invested in restoring the Temple of Olympian Zeus on his visit to Greece.

colonnade called the Stoa.

After leaving Athens, Hadrian visited Delphi, a world center for prophecy and the worship of Apollo. He tried to reform the body governing Delphi, the Amphictyonic Council. Leaving here, on his return to Rome, Hadrian stopped off in Sicily, where he energetically climbed to the top of the great volcano Mount Etna to witness the sunrise.

CHAPTER 4

AN EMPEROR LOVED AND HATED

After ensuring that all was well with his building projects in Rome, Hadrian became the first Roman emperor to assert himself in the African portions of the Roman Empire. Doing so resulted in the loss of a beloved companion and a massive rebellion against his religious policies. Clearly, this was a place where he chose to limit his diplomacy, perhaps because of the contentious history between the Romans and the Judeans or maybe because his grief influenced his approach.

HADRIAN AT HOME

In spring 125 CE, Hadrian was back in Rome. His travels had taken him around most of the empire, and had lasted about four years. At that time, he needed to rest and take stock of what was going on in the capital of the empire. He marked his arrival in Rome by having the gates of the Temple of Janus closed, a seldom-used sign that the Roman world was at peace.

Work on the Pantheon was completed, but other building projects, such as the huge Temple of Rome and Venus, were still ongoing. Hadrian turned his mind to the restoration of the Temple of the Divine Vespasian and Titus in the Forum of Rome. In 126 CE, Hadrian held office as a magistrate in Ostia, the nearby port of Rome, which was rather unusual. Although serving emperors often held political posts such as the consulship in Rome, they seldom became involved in the politics of local communities outside the city. The emperor then devoted some attention to rebuilding the imperial palace on the Palatine Hill and to gaining more public support in Rome itself. A great set of gladiatorial games was held, where 1,835 pairs of fighters put on entertainment for the masses.

Hadrian spent some time out of the city at his estate in Tibur, modern-day Tivoli. Hadrian's Villa is a marvelous site, developed under the watchful eye of the emperor himself. Several buildings were named after sites in Greece such as the Lyceum,

Academy, and Poikile, and the villa also boasts a theater, a stadium, various temples, and libraries for both Greek and Latin books. A section of canal called the Canopus was developed, possibly after Hadrian's trip to Egypt in 130 CE.

In early 127 CE, Hadrian embarked on a tour of northern Italy, spending time in the valley of the Po River. He divided Italy into four separate provinces, each having its own governor, but this eventually proved unpopular and was abolished very soon after his death. He returned to Rome to celebrate the tenth anniversary of his accession to power in the summer of this year. It was then that he allowed himself to be called "father of the country," marking a clear feeling of confidence in his own position and authority at this time.

THE SOUTHERN FRONTIER

In summer 128 CE, Hadrian decided to visit the parts of Africa where Tunisia and Algeria are now, which before this time had never experienced an emperor's personal inspection. In spite of never having been visited, Africa was closer to Rome than many other provinces and had been prosperous and peaceful since the destruction of Carthage in 146 BCE. Perhaps

The Temple of Janus, shown here, was a symbolic structure that indicated much about the state of Rome.

because it was so prosperous and secure, visits by emperors had simply not been needed.

When Hadrian arrived at Carthage, the local people were delighted that it rained, because it had

not done so for five years previously. This was a good omen for the imperial visit. Hearing of the previous water shortage, Hadrian designed a new aqueduct running from the mountains at Zaghouan

This Victorian engraving depicts Hadrian's Villa, located in Tivoli, Italy.

to Carthage. The old Punic city must have fascinated him. Carthage had been razed to the ground and salt ploughed into the fields after Hannibal was defeated. Then it was left abandoned for about one hundred years. After this, the Romans developed it, cutting the top off Byrsa Hill and establishing their own buildings on top of the Punic foundations.

During his visit, Hadrian carried out several important reforms that altered the status of existing settlements, so that it became easier for the inhabitants to acquire full Roman citizenship. Magistrates of so-called *municipia*, or self-governing towns, had held this right before, but at that time it was extended to all town councilors. In addition, several towns that had been municipia were changed to *coloniae*, meaning that all their inhabitants would automatically be Roman citizens and would therefore have improved legal rights, including the right to serve in a Roman legion. Hadrian also awarded ten native communities the status of *municipium*.

By June 128 CE, Hadrian was on his way west to Numidia, where the third legion (Augusta) was stationed at Lambaesis. The commander of the legion was Fabius Catullinus, who was to see the emperor inspect his troops most thoroughly. The army was required to construct certain stretches of limes frontier, though Hadrian again proved to be flexible as to the method of construction, this time deciding to use baked bricks of mud. The limes was used only to guard certain trade routes across the desert and there was no apparent intention to create a continuous physical barrier across the province.

Hadrian approved of the generalship of Catullinus. He praised the soldiers for their building and their maneuvers, but he was critical of some of the cavalry tactics he saw being practiced. Clearly the emperor's praise was genuine, since Catullinus was later promoted to the office of consul in 130 CE. Hadrian made his way west into Mauretania, and sailed back to Rome from Portus Magnus, on the coast of modern-day Algeria. His African trip had only taken a couple of months, and he was getting ready for his last major visit to the eastern empire.

POLITICS AND RELIGION

Hadrian always incorporated a political side to his activities, and one step Hadrian took was to consolidate his army and allocate sufficient numbers of coloniae around the empire so that the legions could be manned by locals where possible. Since the requirement for entry into the Roman army was that soldiers had to be citizens, it made sense to have at least one colonia near each legionary base, so that this condition could be satisfied.

The ruins of a praetorium in Lambaesis (modern-day Tazoult, Algeria).

Hadrian is also known to have held another eastern summit meeting, perhaps in Syria, to discuss Parthia and Armenia. His efforts to secure an eastern peace by diplomacy rather than by force were ongoing from the earlier meeting with the Parthians held in 123 CE, and he helped this one along by first releasing a hostage, the daughter of King Chosroes, as a gesture of good will. It was later said that Hadrian had achieved peace by bribing local chieftains, which may have been true. Hadrian introduced a policy whereby a local city acted within a region as a metropolis, or mother city. Antioch, Tyre, and Damascus were all given this title, which in practice does not seem to have meant much. Hadrian visited other places, including the beautiful city of Petra in the province of Arabia, which was renamed after the emperor.

It was at the beginning of the next year, 130 CE, that Hadrian began to involve himself in Judea, a place that was frequently unwilling to submit to the empire. There had been Jewish rebellions in Cyprus, Egypt, and Libya at the end of Trajan's rule, and since then the Jewish community had not been forgotten by the new emperor.

As Hadrian approached Judea, he formulated some new policies that would create huge problems for him later on. First, there was the prohibition on circumcision, a practice that the Jewish community saw as fundamental to their religion. To the Romans, whose wish was to promote Greek habits and beliefs rather than Jewish ones, circumcision was abhorrent, and they saw it as a mutilation of the body. So it was banned, and the penalty for breaking the law would be death.

Hadrian also proclaimed that Jerusalem would be rebuilt as a colonia of Rome, to be called Aelia Capitolina. "Aelia" was taken from Hadrian's own family name, and "Capitolina" from the name of

This is a view of the Acropolis as seen from the Mouseion, also known as the Hill of the Muses.

the Capitoline Hill in Rome, the center of worship of the god Jupiter. It was to be built and guarded by the tenth legion (Fretensis), which had remained on site since the time of the emperor Titus and the sack of the city in 70 CE. The Jewish holy city was therefore to become a center for the worship of Roman gods and the Roman emperor. There could have been no greater insult to the people of Israel, who began to hate Hadrian with a passion.

THE END OF ANTINOUS

Hadrian's travels in 130 CE took him to Egypt, where he visited the tomb of Pompey the Great, Julius Caesar's great rival. Hadrian rebuilt the tomb and re-erected a statue of the former statesman. Then he moved on to Alexandria, the city at the western Nile delta founded by Alexander the Great. Here he restored the Temple of Serapis, dedicating it in part to himself, as was at that time a normal practice for him. This building had been damaged during the Jewish uprising in 116 CE, so its repair was timely. The emperor visited the Mouseion (Museum), a center for artists, academics, and scientists set up by the great Macedonian king. As may be expected,

Hadrian relished the contact with other intellectuals of his age and entered into many debates where he enjoyed seeing his views prevail. Hadrian and his favorite, Antinous, enjoyed a lion hunt, probably their last. Carvings depicting this event can still be seen in Rome, on the Arch of Constantine.

Hadrian next visited the town of Canopus, famous for its luxury and excess, and then he went on to Heliopolis (City of the Sun) where he saw the temple of the sun god and met a priest called Pancrates. This man may have had considerable influence on the emperor. Hadrian was shown books of spells and witnessed the priest conduct some bizarre rituals, supposedly causing people to have dreams, become sick, and die. Pancrates may well have accompanied Hadrian after this, as the emperor carried on southward up the Nile.

It was on October 24, 130 CE, that a horrible accident occurred that affected Hadrian very deeply. Antinous, his young attendant and lover, died while in the Nile River. Why this happened is not clear. However, the date of the death was significant and may give reason to believe that this was no accident. October 24 marked the occasion when the Egyptian god Osiris had died, also in the Nile.

Osirus was widely seen as ruler of the Underworld, someone who had returned to life after death. Furthermore, Osiris had been identified by some Greeks with Dionysus, a god Hadrian had been fascinated with for years. It was as the new Dionysus that Hadrian had first allowed himself to be worshiped in Ancyra all those years ago when he first became emperor, and he had been fascinated with the worship of Dionysus during his experiences at the Eleusinian Mysteries. It has been suggested that Hadrian was suffering ill health at this stage of his life and that Antinous may have been sacrificed to bring him renewed health. It also has been suggested that Antinous committed suicide, perhaps influenced by what Pancrates or Hadrian wanted him to do. Whatever the truth, Hadrian would never be the same again and would always maintain that the death had been an accident.

MEMORIALIZING THE DEAD

The emperor then set about creating a new city to be called Antinoopolis (City of Antinous) at the site where his lover had died. Was the city built to commemorate the death, or was the death caused because the city was to be founded, to secure its future according to some religious belief? We cannot know the answer. However, despite his state of mind, he was on his travels again within a few days, arriving in Thebes by November 18, 130 CE. The distance involved was about 250 miles (402 km), so Hadrian could not have stayed long to mourn at the site of Antinoopolis. The emperor said that he had seen a star of Antinous rise in the sky and this earned him some mockery.

On his arrival in Thebes, Hadrian wished to visit the singing statue of Pharaoh Amenhotep III, which by some unknown force emitted a singing noise at dawn as the sun's rays began to warm it. On the first day, the statue did not sing to the emperor, which was taken as a bad sign, but then on the second day, it did indeed perform.

Hadrian then returned to Antinoopolis, where he busied himself with the design of the new city. An obelisk was set up to Osiris and the newly deified Antinous, called Osirantinous, asking that the emperor should live to an old age. This could be taken as evidence that Antinous did indeed die with Hadrian's full knowledge in some kind of magic pact. The worship of Antinous spread

ROMAN FUNERALS

Something had to happen to the bodies of the dead. The Roman government was in favor of cremation and

This engraving depicts the grandiose mourning and ceremony for the death of an ancient Roman emperor.

burial, even though the Jewish people of Judea were traditionally in favor of inhumation regardless of what the Roman Empire would impose on them. However, commemorating death in Rome was in a state of change during Hadrian's time, such that in the second century, inhumation was becoming the more prominent choice that would overtake cremation.

In spite of the rise of inhumation, in Hadrian's time, the ritual of burial in ancient Rome involved a procession, cremation and burial, eulogy, feast, and commemoration. The procession was when the deceased's transporters acted to show the status of the deceased, including a number of paid mourners, musicians, mimes, and actors who portrayed ancestral characters from the deceased's family. Cremation and burial was the ceremony in which the body was cremated on the funeral pyre and interred, thus facilitating the deceased's movement across the River Styx. The eulogy was a family's way of expressing the good impression that the deceased left on them or on their surroundings, and the feast closed the funeral for that particular death. Finally, the commemoration offered a periodic opportunity to remember the dead. As was the custom, Hadrian spared few resources to commemorate those who he truly cared for.

across the Roman Empire very quickly, extending to Greece, Asia Minor, and close to Rome itself, where a temple for Antinous was set up in Lanuvium in Latium. In April 131 CE a set of games was held in Antinoopolis, which Hadrian probably attended in person. A festival was held at the same time in Alexandria to commemorate the death of Paulina, Hadrian's sister, who had also died recently. It was distasteful to many to see that Hadrian's sister merited only a set of games, whereas his young lover had a complete city built as a memorial.

This lithograph depicts the Colossi of Memnon, one of which came to be known as the singing statue of Pharaoh Amenhotep III after an earthquake in 27 BCE.

AN EMPEROR IN FAVOR

Hadrian returned to Syria and Antioch, stopping at many other cities on the way. His route of travel is hard to identify exactly, but we know that he spent the winter in Athens, contributing further benefactions to the city. He held games in the stadium, where beast hunts were put on for the people's pleasure and one thousand animals were slaughtered. The dedication of the shrine to Olympian Zeus was finally accomplished and a huge statue of the god made of gold and ivory was uncovered. The Athenians, in recognition of the emperor's kindness, erected a statue of him behind the new temple. A gymnasium was opened near the city center, as was Hadrian's new library, with one hundred columns of Libyan marble supporting it.

The Temple of Olympian Zeus was to act as the center for the new Panhellenion, the festival and focus for all things Greek. Hadrian wanted to hold the event every four years, and he also planned to use the new sanctuary for other large public events in the years between festivals. As a gesture of thanks to him, the people of Athens erected Hadrian's Gate, an archway into the city bearing the inscription "This is the city of Hadrian, not Theseus."

By late spring of the year 132 CE, the tired emperor was ready to return to Rome, but events would not yet permit this to happen.

BAR KOKHBA'S REBELLION

News arrived in Athens of a rebellion in Judea that gradually increased in its intensity. Acting against the various forms of religious suppression that the Jewish community endured soon left the whole of Judea in ferment. The leader of the revolt was one Bar Kokhba, also known as Shim'on. His name seems to have meant "son of a star," and he proclaimed himself the prince of Israel. He was hostile to both Romans and Christians.

Hadrian returned to the province to take care of things personally, but he also summoned his top general, Sextus Julius Severus, governor of Britain, to lead the Roman troops. In this extraordinary campaign, Hadrian achieved one of his most difficult and bloody conquests after three years of insurgency. The emperor returned to Rome for the last time, first taking a route northward to the

After being defeated, the Jewish people who survived the massacre were expelled from Judea in 135 CE.

Danube River, where he may have met to confer with Severus. Hadrian undertook a major drive to recruit more soldiers into the army from all across the empire to deal with the rebellion. Many people died on both sides of the conflict, one source claiming over half a million Jewish deaths. Eventually, in 135 CE, Bar Kokhba was killed and his head was paraded in front of the Romans. Severus and his aide Publicius Marcellus were given triumphal honors in recognition of their success, an award rarely given to anyone other than the emperor. The ban on circumcision was not lifted, and the new temple of Hadrian that arose in Aelia Capitolina remained a source of resentment.

CHAPTER 5

WHAT HADRIAN LEFT BEHIND

Hadrian's legacy was carefully crafted throughout his lifetime, such that he left the Roman Empire very different than he found it. His legacy, along with the ways he enriched the lives of his people, clearly demonstrates why he is considered one of the Five Good Emperors.

THE LAST GREAT BUILDING PROJECT

On his return to Rome, Hadrian worked on one of his last building projects, his mausoleum. The first emperor, Augustus, had built a large, circular monument for himself in Rome that his ashes and the ashes of succeeding emperors had been put in, up to and including the emperor Nerva. When Trajan died it had been deemed proper to insert his ashes into a column he had built. So for the

The Bridge of Hadrian leads across the Tiber River to Hadrian's mausoleum, where he was laid to rest after his death in 138 CE.

first time, there was no obvious place for Hadrian's remains to be stored, unless he built one. Bearing in mind the size of the earlier emperor's resting place, Hadrian built a monument of almost exactly the same external dimensions on the opposite side of the river Tiber from the Mausoleum of Augustus. It was his last great building project. Leading across the Tiber to the mausoleum, now called the Castel Sant'Angelo, Hadrian built a bridge called the Aelian Bridge, now called the Ponte Sant'Angelo. The mausoleum lies on the right bank of the Tiber, and the Aelian Bridge crosses the Tiber River east of modern-day Vatican City.

There are many monuments built by Hadrian that still stand. The Pantheon is Hadrian's most beautiful building and the largest intact Roman building in the world. The great wall in northern England is another monument to this emperor's passion for building. All over the Roman world we can revisit Hadrian by looking at his monuments. The villa at Tivoli, containing a number of replicas of monuments and buildings that the emperor had seen on his travels, including the Terrace of the Tempe and the Canopus, is evocative of his devotion to architecture.

HADRIAN'S TRAVELS

Hadrian's journeys are remarkable by anyone's standards. He is known to have traveled in almost every province of the empire, a feat unequalled by any other emperor. Of greater lasting impact is the fact that almost everywhere he went he either built something or held games. It was as if he found inspiration in all of the places he visited.

The basic outline of Hadrian's journeys includes a span of forty-four years of continuous traveling, for a total distance of 40,000 miles (64,373 km). His travels before becoming the Roman emperor in 117 CE included business visits to his family's estates and travel as an attendant or official under the service of Trajan. As the emperor, however, the purpose of his travels became about securing the frontiers and interior of the empire, beautifying different areas, and his own personal tourism.

CHOOSING AN HEIR

After his final return to Rome, around 136 CE, Hadrian's health started to deteriorate, probably because of a heart condition. He began to suffer from nosebleeds and other problems, and this made him turn his mind to who would succeed him. Some of his advisers considered the issue and Pedanius Fuscus, his sister Paulina's grandson, was their preferred choice. There was a disagreement among the advisers, however, and perhaps a plot. Fuscus was implicated and put to death. Servianus, his grandfather and Hadrian's ninety-year-old brother-in-law, was forced to commit suicide for having supported Fuscus. This brought great shame and disrepute on the emperor, since Servianus had served Rome loyally for many years and in many different conflicts.

Hadrian spoke of the advantages of adoption, saying that the selection of an heir by this method was preferable to passing on power to a natural son. However, he seems to have become suspicious of all those around him, and he began to detest many of his former friends. He appointed Lucius Ceionius Commodus his heir, calling him Aelius Caesar, but this man was already ill himself, vomiting blood regularly, and died at the end of 137 CE.

At the same time, the empress Sabina died. It is not likely that her husband greatly mourned her passing. It was even rumored that he poisoned her.

At the beginning of 138 CE, Hadrian announced publicly that he was ill and also that he had adopted Aurelius Antoninus as his successor. Taking an even longer view, Hadrian appointed two younger men to be next in line to the throne after Antoninus. They were Lucius Aurelius Commodus, son of Aelius Caesar, and Marcus Aurelius Verus, who later became the emperor Marcus Aurelius. Marcus had been a favorite of Hadrian for some time, and he was thought to have been preferred above all others by the emperor. It was probably just his youth that prevented him from being nominated first heir.

HADRIAN'S DEATH

Hadrian had been cursed by old Servianus, who had wished him a dreadful death. The bitter curse seemed to take effect. He wanted his life to end, but no one would help him. His doctors refused

This bust of Sabina, Hadrian's wife, was created circa 100 CE, around the time they were first married.

to administer a lethal drug and Mastor, his Hungarian master of the hunt, would not help him die either. His state of mind became more disturbed as he waited for death, and he removed from power Marcius Turbo, his most loyal of lieutenants and prefect of the city.

Hadrian embarked on a final journey from Rome to the Bay of Naples, where the mild climate would be less oppressive for him in his last days. He finally died on July 10, 138 CE, cursing his doctors. He was hated by all at the time of his death, probably because both the beginning and the end of his reign were marred by the assassinations of popular public figures. He was deified by the Roman people only because the emperor Aurelius Antoninus, who would become known as Antoninus Pius, insisted on it. Hadrian wrote a poem shortly before he died, and he dedicated it to his soul. It has been translated here as a fitting end to the story of his life.

Small soul, wandering, sweet,
Guest of the body, companion,
Where will you go now? To places
Pale, harsh, clouded,
Nor, as you do normally, will you make any jokes.

CONTEMPORARY MEMORIES OF HADRIAN

There are many reasons that Hadrian was remembered. He was tall, elegant, and had a full head of curly hair, with his Greek-style beard the most distinguishing of his features. He would've been considered quite handsome.

He was also highly intelligent and very well educated. He enjoyed debate with scholars from all walks of life, though he could not stand losing an argument. He numbered several philosophers among his friends, such as Epictetus and Heliodorus, though it seems that in old age he may have had less respect for intellectuals than when he was young. He claimed that he did not enjoy upsetting people in argument, although he felt that mocking teachers of the arts was acceptable.

His passion for all things Greek did not meet with universal approval among his Roman subjects. In his personal life, he met with problems from having intimate relationships with both men and married women, neither of which was acceptable in Roman society.

The emperor also bore grudges and remembered arguments for years after they occurred. He was prone to allowing his friends to fall out of favor, and toward the end of his life he treated several old acquaintances particularly badly.

Along with the buildings he left behind, Hadrian made many social reforms, including those that secured the authority of the Senate and the safety of the people. In his reforms of the army Hadrian created precedents for the empire that would last for many generations. His establishment of extra coloniae, providing a source of Roman citizens for recruitment into the armies, was crucial to the empire's later stability, and allowed more people to become involved directly in government. Hadrian increased the rights of citizens in municipia and this, too, promoted stability.

In many ways he was an ideal emperor, because he cared about the long-term future of the Roman world. Yet it seems that his diffidence made it hard for people to like and trust him. He was always careful to ensure the loyalty of those around him, if necessary by spying on them and interrogating them in person. He was respected but not liked or trusted by many of those around him.

ROME WITHOUT HADRIAN

Aurelius Antoninus, the next of the Five Good Emperors, succeeded Hadrian. His rule was largely peaceful. At the outset of his reign he incurred criticism by insisting that Hadrian be deified, and it was this loyalty to his predecessor that gained him the name Antoninus Pius (meaning pious, or respectful). There were few major wars in his reign, but campaigns in northern Britain led to the northward extension of the frontier from Hadrian's Wall and the establishment of the so-called Antonine Wall. Antoninus Pius was popular, and the empire was perhaps at its most stable under his leadership. He died in 161 CE.

He was succeeded by Lucius Aurelius Commodus, who died in 169 CE after ruling for nine years as joint emperor with Marcus Aurelius. Hadrian had required Antoninus Pius to adopt him as third in line to the throne in 138 CE.

During the reign of Marcus Aurelius Verus, problems arose on various frontiers, including Britain, Germany, and in the eastern empire. A campaign north of the Danube followed and the Romans suffered a defeat at the hands of the Ger-

This engraving by Victor Duruy from 1884 depicts Antoninus Pius, the next of the Five Good Emperors after Hadrian.

manic Marcomanni tribe in 170 CE. They took vengeance on the Marcomanni two years later, and their victory was commemorated on the Column of Marcus Aurelius, or Colonna. The area north of

This engraving depicts a battle between the German Marcomanni forces and Roman Empire soldiers.

the Danube was to cause more problems for Marcus Aurelius, and the emperor died here in 180 CE, handing power over to his son Commodus.

Thus would be the end of the Five Good Emperors, the final two leaving an impact that rivaled Hadrian's and would last until the fall of the Roman Empire.

colonia A Roman town or settlement, where all the inhabitants had the status of full Roman citizens.

consul The title given to a very senior Roman magistrate, a man who had reached the top of the cursus honorum.

consul ordinarius A title given to each of the two consuls whose term started off a new year.

cursus honorum Name given to the Roman political career ladder.

eponymous archon A leading magistrate in Athens who presided over significant events, acting in the same way as a leading town councilor or mayor.

imperator The title given to a conquering general.

magistracy An official position for a young man making his way along the cursus honorum.

military tribune A term given to a variety of different officials in Roman society, simply meaning a magistrate, or official who was chosen to serve for one year with the army.

municipium A town that had self-governing status and whose officials became Roman citizens.

patricians The ruling classes.

praetor A title given to a senior Roman magistrate, a man who had almost reached the top of the cursus honorum.

princeps Meaning "first citizen," a title that came into use at the time of Augustus, the first proper emperor of Rome. The princeps shared his authority with the Senate, though he was in effect the decision maker in most affairs.

Punic The people of ancient Carthage, the place, or something related to or from there.

quaestor Another magistracy, this one involved a year of financial management within the Roman civil service that could lead to election into the Senate.

republic The term often used for the Roman state, represented by the acronym SPQR, both during the period of representational government that preceded Rome's empire and after.

Senate A body of about six hundred senior statesmen whose authority combined with the emperor's to act as the lawgiver of Rome.

sesterces A large bronze coin used as currency during ancient Roman times.

suffect consul A senior Roman magistrate who was elected to replace a deceased consul ordinarius until the end of the year-long term.

toga A woolen garment worn by Romans.

tribune of the people A variety of different officials in Roman society who were originally chosen to represent the people's interests against exploitation by patricians. In imperial times the post had become much more of a formality.

vigintivir One of twenty magistrates in Rome, usually picked from young noblemen embarking on their cursus honorum.

The American Institute for Roman Culture
1101 W. 34th St.
Suite 730-174
Austin, TX 78705
Phone: (512) 772-1844
http://romanculture.org
This organization offers various opportunities and resources for learning about Rome's cultural heritage.

Canadian War Museum
1 Vimy Place
Ottawa, ON K1A 0M8
Canada
Phone: 1-800-555-5621
http://www.warmuseum.ca
This museum's collection holds archives, library materials, and artifacts to learn about ancient and modern warfare. I

The J. Paul Getty Museum
1200 Getty Center Drive
Los Angeles, CA 90049-1687
Phone: (310) 440-7330
http://www.getty.edu/museum
This museum exhibits and conserves collections of historically significant art. Of particular interest to ancient Rome are the mosaics that once decorated public and private spaces of the Roman Empire.

The Metropolitan Museum of Art
1000 Fifth Avenue
New York, NY 10028
Phone: 212-535-7710
http://www.metmuseum.org
Visit this museum's Roman gallery to view classical art of the ancient Roman Empire. Volunteer-led tours also guide visitors to the highlights of the Met's collections.

Museum of Fine Arts Boston
Avenue of the Arts
465 Huntington Avenue
Boston, Massachusetts 02115
Phone: (617) 267-9300
http://www.mfa.org
This museum hosts and facilitates various school and community programs in the arts and holds events and tours in its galleries. The Art of the Ancient World galleries and collections offer a glimpse into the past of the creativity of ancient civilizations.

Royal Ontario Museum
100 Queen's Park,
Toronto, ON M5S 2C6
Canada
Phone: (416) 586-8000
http://www.rom.on.ca
This museum's Eaton Gallery of Rome offers art and archi-

tectural remains of the Roman Empire, and its library and archives enable research into the non-circulating arts and archaeology materials.

University of Pennsylvania Museum of Archaeology and Anthropology
3260 South Street
Philadelphia, PA 19104
Phone: (215) 898-4000
http://www.penn.museum
This museum's Rome Gallery contains statues, jewelry, art, and other artifacts of the Roman world. Or, search their collections online for different objects, places, materials, time periods, and other attributes.

WEBSITES

Because of the changing nature of internet links, Rosen Publishing has developed an online list of websites related to the subject of this book. This site is updated regularly. Please use this link to access this list:

http://www.rosenlinks.com/LANW/hadrian

Allan, Tony. *Exploring the Life, Myth, and Art of Ancient Rome* (Civilizations of the World). New York, NY: Rosen Publishing, 2012.

Anderson, Marilyn. *Ancient Rome* (Ancient Civilizations). New York, NY: Rosen Publishing, 2012.

Beard, Mary. *SPQR: A History of Ancient Rome*. New York, NY: Liveright, 2016.

Hingley, Richard. *Hadrian's Wall: A Life*. Oxford, UK: Oxford University Press, 2015.

Garnsey, Peter, and Richard Saller. *The Roman Empire: Economy, Society and Culture*. 2nd ed. Berkeley, CA: University of California Press, 2014.

Lateiner, Donald, Barbara K. Gold, and Judith Perkins, eds. *Roman Literature, Gender and Reception: Domina Illustris* (Routledge Monographs in Classical Studies). Abingdon, UK: Routledge, 2013.

Lefkowitz, Mary R., and Maureen B. Fant, eds. *Women's Life in Greece and Rome: A Source Book in Translation*. 4th ed. London, UK: Bloomsbury, 2016.

Levithan, Josh. *Roman Siege Warfare*. Ann Arbor, MI: University of Michigan Press, 2013.

Opper, Thorsten. *Hadrian: Art, Politics and Economy* (British Museum Research Publication). London, UK: British Museum Press, 2013.

Potter, David. *The Emperors of Rome: The Story of Imperial Rome from Julius Caesar to the Last Emperor*. London, UK: Quercus Publishing, 2016.

Saliola, Marco, and Fabrizio Casprini. *Pugio—Gladius Brevis Est: History and Technology of the Roman Battle Dagger* (BAR International Series 2404). Oxford, UK: British Archaeological Reports, 2012.

Travis, John Robert, and Hilary Travis. *Roman Shields: Historical Development and Reconstruction*. Amberly, UK: Amberley Publishing, 2014.

Ancientcoins.biz. "Roman Economy—Prices in Ancient Rome." November 15, 2003. http://web.archive.org/web/20070113183811/http://www.ancientcoins.biz/pages/economy/.

Birley, Anthony R. *Hadrian, the Restless Emperor*. London, UK: Routledge, 1997.

Boatwright, Mary Taliaferro. *Hadrian and the City of Rome*. Princeton, NJ: University Press, 1987.

Bowman, Alan, *The Cambridge Ancient History, Volume XI*. Cambridge, UK: Cambridge University Press, 2000.

Claridge, Amanda. *Rome*. Oxford, UK: Oxford University Press, 1998.

Davenport, Caillan, and Christopher Mallan. "Hadrian's Adoption Speech in Cassius Dio's Roman History and the Problems of Imperial Succession." *American Journal of Philology*, Volume 135, Number 4 (Winter 2014). pp. 637-668. http://espace.library.uq.edu.au/view/UQ:346457/UQ346457_OA.pdf.

Dio Cassius. *Lives of the Later Caesars*. London, UK: Penguin, 1976.

Dio Cassius. *Roman History, Books 61 to 70*. Cambridge, UK: Loeb Classical Library, 2000.

Fife, Steven. "The Roman Funeral." Ancient History Encyclopedia, January 18, 2012. www.ancient.eu/article/96/.

Horbury, William. *Jewish War under Trajan and Hadrian*. Cambridge, UK: Cambridge University Press, 2014.

Kulikowski, Michael. *Imperial Triumph: The Roman World from Hadrian to Constantine*. London, UK: Profile Books, 2016.

Lambert, Royston. *Beloved and God: The Story of Hadrian and Antinous*. London, UK: Weidenfeld and Nicolson, 1984.

McKeown, J. "The Cursus Honorum." Etrusia, October 21 2004. http://romans.etrusia.co.uk/romans_cursus_honorum.php.

Morwood, James. *Hadrian*. London, UK: Bloomsbury, 2013.

Perowne, Stewart. *Hadrian*. New York, NY: W. W. Norton, 1962.

I

J

L

M

N

O

ABOUT THE AUTHORS

Beatriz Santillian earned her BA in English in 2009 and her MA in history in 2012. She is a fan of ancient history and loves to learn about artifacts from the past. Santillian writes on topics about culture, technology, and change, and she also writes software in her spare time. She lives in Rochester, New York, with her daughter.

Julian Morgan earned his BA in Greek studies at Bristol University, England, in 1979. He also earned a master's degree in computers and education at King's College, London, in 1990. He is currently head of classics at Derby Grammar School. Morgan has a special interest in software design and has published many programs, including ROMANA and Rome the Eternal City, through his business, J-PROGS. He is a member of the American Classical League's Committee on Educational Computer Applications. He is the computing coordinator for the Joint Association of Classical Teaching (JACT) and has a regular column, Computanda, in their bulletin. He also runs a training business called Medusa that specializes in helping teachers of classics use information technology in their teaching.

PHOTO CREDITS

Cover, p. 3 Gilmanshin/Shutterstock.com; cover (background) Santi Rodriguez/Shutterstock.com; pp. 6 (left), 92 Alinari Archives/Getty Images; p. 6 (center) Lefteris Papaulakis/Shutterstock.com; pp. 6 (right), 7 (left, right) Kamira/Shutterstock.com; p. 13 De Agostini Picture Library/De Agostini Editorial/Getty Images; pp. 16–17 Eric Vandeville/Gamma-Rapho/Getty Images; pp. 18–19, 78–79, 98–99 Universal History Archive/Universal Images Group/Getty Images; p. 23 Hulton Archive/Getty Images; p. 26 1911/iStock/Thinkstock; p. 30 Peter Hermes Furian/Shutterstock.com; p. 34 Imagno/Hulton Fine Art Collection/Getty Images; p. 39 Sementer/Shutterstock.com; pp. 40–41 © North Wind Picture Archives; p. 43 age fotostock/Alamy Stock Photo; p. 47 Roland Ackermann/iStock/Thinkstock; pp. 50–51 Juliane Jacobs/iStock/Thinkstock; p. 55 Mondadori Portfolio/Antonio Quattrone/Bridgeman Images; p. 57 ZU 09/E+/Getty Images; pp. 60–61 photo stella/Shutterstock.com; pp. 64–65 adoc-photos/Corbis Historical/Getty Images; pp. 66–67 Antiqueimages/Alamy Stock Photo; pp. 70–71 De Agostini/C. Sappa/De Agostini Picture Library/Getty Images; pp. 72–73 Bernard Cox/Bridgeman Images; pp. 80–81 Private Collection/De Agostini Picture Library/Bridgeman Images; p. 84 Culture Club/Hulton Archive/Getty Images; pp. 86–87 Kiev.Victor/Shutterstock.com; p. 97 © Look and Learn/Bridgeman Images; interior pages background images © iStockphoto.com/kikkalek5050 (sky), Triff/Shutterstock.com (map).

Designer: Brian Garvey; Editor: Bernadette Davis; Photo Researcher: Karen Huang